Sounds
Interesting

The Science of Acoustics

by Dr. David Darling

 DILLON PRESS
New York

Maxwell Macmillan Canada
Toronto

Maxwell Macmillan International
New York Oxford Singapore Sydney

Photographic Acknowledgments

The photographs are reproduced through the courtesy of Unicorn Stock Photos/Chris Brown, Richard Dippold, A. Gunmankin, Ron P. Jaffe, Fred D. Jordan, Dennis MacDonald, MacDonald Photography, Jim Riddle, and Aneal Vohra.

Library of Congress Cataloging-in-Publication Data
Darling, David J.
    Sounds interesting : the science of acoustics / by David Darling.
        p. cm. — (Experiment!)
    Includes index.
    Summary: Demonstrates the principles of sound and the science of acoustics through a variety of experiments.
    ISBN 0-87518-477-4
    1. Acoustics—Juvenile literature. 2. Sounds——Juvenile literature. 3. Animal sounds—Juvenile literature.
    [1. Acoustics—Experiments. 2. Sound—Experiments. 3. Experiments.] I. Title. II. Series: Darling, David J. Experiment!
QC225.5.D37 1991
534—dc20   91-4002

Dillon Press
Macmillan Publishing Company
866 Third Avenue
New York, NY 10022

Maxwell Macmillan Canada, Inc.
1200 Eglinton Avenue East
Suite 200
Don Mills, Ontario M3C 3N1

Macmillan Publishing Company is part of the Maxwell Communication Group of Companies.

First edition
Printed in the United States of America
10 9 8 7 6 5 4 3 2 1

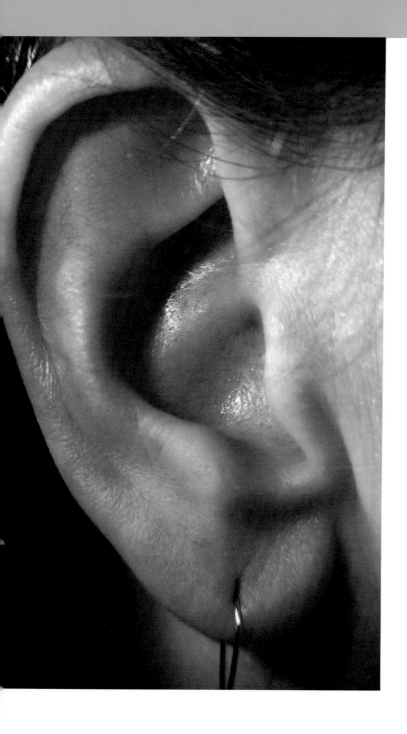

Contents

What Is Science?

Imagine gazing to the edge of the universe with the help of a giant telescope, or designing a future car using a computer that can do over a billion calculations a second. Think what it would be like to investigate the strange calls of the humpback whale, dig up the bones of a new type of dinosaur, or drill a hole ten miles into the earth.

As you read this, men and women around the world are doing exactly these things. Others are trying to find out how the human brain works, how to build better rocket engines, and how to develop new energy sources for the twenty-first century. There are researchers working at the South Pole, in the Amazon jungle,

under the sea, in space, and in laboratories on every continent. All these people are scientists. But what does that mean? Just what is science?

Observation

Science is simply a way of looking at the world with an open, inquiring mind. It usually starts with an observation. For example, you might observe that the leaves of some trees turn brown, yellow, or red in fall. That may seem obvious. But to a scientist, it raises all sorts of interesting questions. What substances in a leaf cause the various colors? What happens when the color changes? Does the leaf swap its green-colored chemical for a brown one? Or are the chemicals that cause the fall colors there all the time but remain hidden from view when the green substance is present?

Hypothesis

At this stage, you might come up with your own explanation for what is going on inside the leaf. This early explanation–a sort of intelligent guess–is called a working hypothesis. To be useful, a hypothesis should lead to predictions that can be tested. For instance, your hypothesis might be that leaves always contain brown, yellow, or red chemicals. It is just that when the green substance is there it masks or covers over the other colors. This is a good scientific hypothesis because a test can be done that could prove it wrong.

Experiment

As a next step, you might devise an experiment to look more deeply into the problem. A well-designed experiment allows you to isolate the factors you think are important, while controlling or leaving out the rest.

Somehow you have to extract the colored chemicals from a batch of green

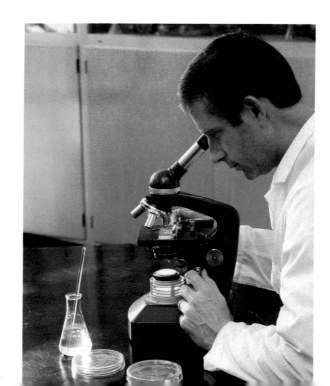

leaves and those from a batch of brown leaves. You might do this, for example, by crushing the leaves and putting a drop of "leaf juice" partway up a narrow strip of blotting paper. Hanging the blotting paper so that it dips in a bowl of water would then cause different colored chemicals from the leaf to be carried to different heights up the paper. By comparing the blotting paper records from the green leaves and the brown leaves, you would be able to tell which chemicals were the same and which were different. Then, depending on the results, you could conclude either that your first hypothesis seemed right or that it needed to be replaced.

Real Science

What we have just described is perhaps the "standard" or "ideal" way to do science. But just as real houses are never spotlessly clean, real science is never quite as neat and tidy as we might wish. Experiments and investigations do not always go the

way scientists expect. Being human, scientists cannot control all the parts of an experiment. Sometimes they are surprised by the results, and often important discoveries are made completely by chance.

Breakthroughs in science do not even have to begin with an observation of the outside world. Albert Einstein, for instance, used "thought experiments" as the starting point for his greatest pieces of work—the special and general theories of relativity. One of his earliest thought experiments was to imagine what it would be like to ride on a light beam. The fact is, scientists use all sorts of different approaches, depending on the problem and the circumstances.

Some important things, however, are common to all science. First, scientists must always be ready to admit mistakes or that their knowledge is incomplete. Scientific ideas are thrown out and replaced if they no longer agree with what is observed. There is no final "truth" in science—only an ongoing quest for better and better explanations of the real world.

Second, all good experiments must be able to be repeated so that other scientists can check the results. It is always possible to make an error, especially in a complicated experiment. So, it is essential that other people, in other places, can perform the same experiment to see if they agree with the findings.

Third, to be effective, science must be shared. In other words, scientists from all over the world must exchange their ideas and results freely through journals and meetings. Not only that, but the general public must be kept informed of what scientists are doing so that they, too, can help to shape the future of scientific research.

To become a better scientist yourself is quite simple. Keep an open mind, ask lots of questions, and most important of all—experiment!

CHAPTER 1

Good Vibrations

The world is full of sound—a dog's bark, the wail of a police siren, the chatter of students in a classroom. Even when everything outside is quiet, you can still hear your own breathing and the steady beating of your heart.

Sound is one of the most important ways we have of sensing our surroundings and communicating with other people. Sometimes it can be a nuisance, as when an airplane or a car roars by. Then we call it noise. On the other hand, many sounds, such as those of musical instruments, are extremely pleasant.

Sounds come in every variety imaginable. But what exactly *is* sound? How is it made and how does it travel?

◄ *The sounds produced during a thunderstorm are among the loudest in nature.*

Sound Energy

Sound is a form of energy. This fact becomes most clear when a loud sound causes something nearby to rattle or move about. For example, if a television set or a record player is turned up high, the sound from it may cause small objects in the same room to shake.

Sound energy is produced by anything that moves back and forth. A mosquito's wings, for instance, beat back and forth very rapidly. This causes similar back-and-forth movements, or vibrations, in the surrounding air. When the air vibrations reach our ears we hear the mosquito's familiar hum.

A "Sound Gun"

You Will Need:

- A cardboard tube
- Plastic wrap
- A nail
- A birthday-cake candle
- Matches
- A dish
- Some sand

What to Do:
Cover both ends of the tube with plastic wrap. Make sure that the plastic is stretched tight. Use the nail to make a small hole in the middle of the plastic at one end. Put some sand in the dish and stand the candle upright in the sand. Light the candle. Hold the "sound gun" so that the hole is about 1" from the candle flame. Tap the plastic at the other end of the tube with your finger. What do you hear? What happens to the flame? Try to explain your observations.

Plastic wrap

Hole

Small candle

Sand

Warning: Always be careful when using matches. If in doubt ask an adult for help.

◄ *This drawing shows how to conduct your own "sound gun" experiment.*

Making Waves

You Will Need:

- A Slinky toy
- A broom handle or other long round pole
- Two chairs
- A long jump rope

What to Do:

Thread the coils of the Slinky on to the broom handle. Rest the broom handle across the backs of the two chairs, as shown. Hold the Slinky by both ends and pull it apart, without stretching it too far. Jerk one end slightly. Observe how the coils of the Slinky move. Jerk one end hard, then more gently. Notice what happens in each case.

Hold one end of the jump rope and ask a friend to hold the other end. Shake your end of the rope once. Shake it hard and then more gently. What do you observe?

The Slinky and the jump rope behave like a length of air. When you jerk or shake one end, you set up a vibration. The way the Slinky and jump rope move is similar to the way air moves when an object vibrates nearby.

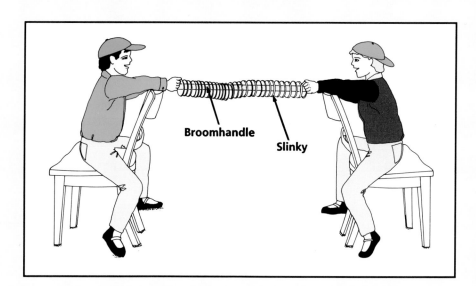

Broomhandle

Slinky

◀ What does the Slinky in this experiment demonstrate about the way air moves?

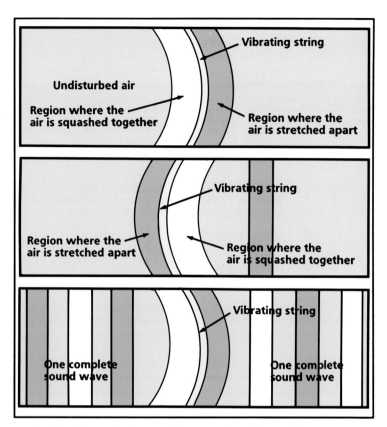

▲ *A vibrating string pushes and pulls on the air around it.*

Pushes and Pulls in the Air

The air next to a vibrating object is alternately squeezed together and pulled apart as the object moves back and forth. This causes the air farther away to be squeezed together and pulled apart, too.

You can picture how this works by thinking about a long line of people, in which each person is holding on to the shoulders of his or her neighbor in front. If the person at the very back suddenly pushes forward, a wave of pushes travels down the line. If the same person pulls back, a wave of pulls is set in motion. The bigger the starting push or pull, the bigger the wave that spreads out. In the same way, an object makes a louder sound if its vibrations are large than if they are small.

Sound and Matter

Sound waves do not only travel through air. In water, sound can be heard over great distances. Whales, for example, seem to be able to communicate with each other underwater even if they are tens or perhaps hundreds of miles apart.

Sound can also pass easily through hard materials such as metal, stone, bone, wood, and glass. Soft substances, however, including fabric and rubber, quickly absorb sound waves. They can be used to

Something to Travel Through

You Will Need:

- A stone
- A tuning fork
- Two plastic cups
- Fine string
- Scissors
- A tape measure
- Coarse string*
- Fishing line or nylon thread*
- A portable tape recorder*

What to Do:

Stand with your ear next to a brick wall. Ask a friend to tap on the wall some distance away. Can you hear anything? Can you hear the tapping if your ear is not pressed to the wall? If so, does it sound the same?

Strike the tuning fork and hold it just in front of your chin. Listen. Strike it again and press the rounded end of the tuning fork against your chin. Listen once more. Is the sound louder, quieter, or about the same? Try to explain your results by thinking about how the vibrations of the tuning fork are carried to your ear.

The next time you are in a swimming pool or a bath, lie back so that your ears are underwater. Can you hear anything? If so, how is that possible?

▲ What do you hear when a friend taps a brick wall some distance away?

Note: Items marked "*" are used only in the "Taking It Further" part of an experiment.

continued on next page

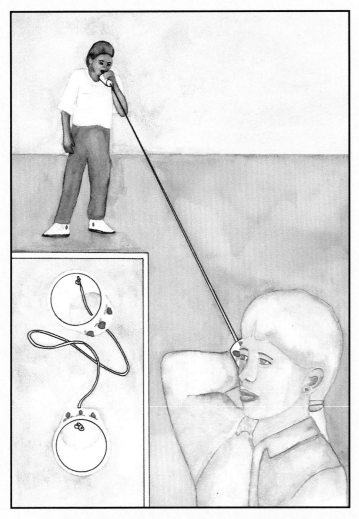

▲ *What do you hear through your cup and string "telephone"?*

Make a hole in the bottom of each plastic cup. Cut off a length of about 30' of fine string. Push one end of the string through the hole in one cup and the other end through the hole in the other cup. Knot the string to stop it from coming out of the holes. Stand facing a friend and pull the string tight. Hold your cup to your ear while your friend talks slowly and clearly into the other cup. What do you hear? What happens if you let the string go slack?

***Taking It Further*:**
Record a passage from a book on the tape recorder. Hold your cup to your ear while your friend holds the other cup to the loudspeaker of the tape recorder. Again, keep the string tightly stretched. Repeat the experiment using a 30' length of fishing line instead of fine string. Does this affect the quality of what you hear? Can you explain your results? Repeat the experiment using coarse string. Again, describe your findings.

deaden the noise of a car engine or prevent echoes in a concert hall.

The one thing that no sound can travel through is empty space. So, when astronauts visited the moon they had to communicate using radios. Only by touching helmets would they have been able to talk to one another directly. This would have allowed the vibrations of their voices to pass through the material of their helmets.

Sometimes you will see movies in which spacecraft make noises when their engines are fired or they are hit by the enemy. But, in truth, all such action would be completely silent from outside.

Echo, Echo

When sound waves strike a hard, solid object, such as the side of a building, they bounce back. That is, they are reflected. A softer surface, however, soaks up most of the energy in the sound wave and reflects very little. This explains why sounds in a

On the moon where there is no air, astro- ▶
nauts had to communicate using radios.

Radio waves transmitted from ship

Radio waves reflected back to ship from school of fish

▲ *This drawing shows how sound waves from a ship can be used to locate fish.*

bare room appear very loud, but in a room with carpeting, curtains, and soft furnishings, sounds are more muffled.

A sound that bounces back is called an echo. If you stand a long distance away from a large wall or a steep mountain and shout, your calls will return to you a short time later. The farther you are from the reflecting surface, the longer is the gap between making the call and hearing the echo. Why do you think this should be?

Ships and submarines use beams of sound to measure the depth of water, to chart the seabed, and to find shoals of fish. The system is called sonar, which stands for sound navigation and ranging. A device under the hull sends out regular pulses of sound. These bounce off the seabed or off shoals of fish and return to the ship. After the echoes have been picked up, they are turned into a picture on a screen.

Bouncing Sounds Around

You Will Need:

- **Two long cardboard tubes**
- **A ticking watch**
- **A wall**

What to Do:

Ask a friend to hold one of the tubes at an angle to the wall with the ticking watch at the other end of the tube. Hold the other tube to your ear and aim it at the same spot on the wall as your friend's tube is pointing. Can you hear anything? If not, alter the angle your tube makes with the wall (still pointing at the same spot). Is there anything special about the position at which you can hear the watch? What does this tell you about what is happening to the sound waves when they hit the wall?

▲ *What angle of the tubes works best to hear the watch ticking?*

CHAPTER 2

Sounds Different

Listen to a piece of your favorite music and notice how the sound changes from one moment to the next. As well as going from loud to soft, it also varies in pitch. Pitch is the highness or lowness of a sound. A bass guitar, for instance, makes notes of a very low pitch. A lead guitar, on the other hand, can play over a wider range from low to very high notes.

The pitch of a sound depends on how quickly the source of the sound is vibrating. The faster the vibrations, the higher the sound.

▼ *Different instruments in a rock band make sounds that vary in pitch.*

Higher and Higher

You Will Need:

- **Nylon fishing line**
- **A piece of wood about 1" thick, 2" wide, and 3' long**
- **Two thin pieces of wood about 1" long**
- **A nail**
- **A hammer**
- **A plastic toy bucket**
- **Sand**
- **Kitchen scales or other type of balance**
- **A piano or other tuned musical instrument***

What to Do:

Hammer the nail firmly into one end of the large piece of wood. Tie one end of the fishing line to the nail. Place the wood on a table and pull the fishing line over the wood so that it hangs over the side of the table. Tie the bucket to the end of the line. Place the two small pieces of wood under the line as shown. Pluck the line and listen to the note. Put some sand in the bucket and pluck the line again. Is the note higher, lower, or the same? Add some more sand. Has the pitch gone up or down?

Without changing the amount of sand in the bucket, move the two small pieces of wood closer together.

◀ *What do you hear when you pluck the fishing line tied at one end to the bucket?*

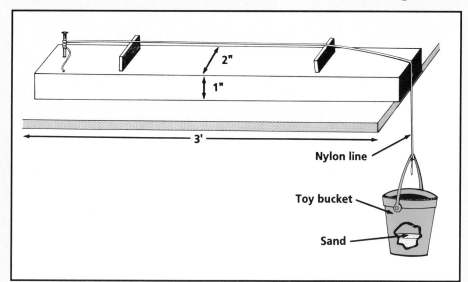

2"

1"

3'

Nylon line

Toy bucket

Sand

continued on next page

What happens to the pitch? Can you explain your findings?

***Taking It Further*:**
You will need the help of someone who can play an instrument (such as a piano, recorder, or guitar). The instrument must be in tune.

Begin by tuning the nylon line to a particular note. Do this by putting a bit of sand in the bucket and then moving one of the small pieces of wood until the note made by the line matches a note on the instrument. Weigh the bucket and sand. Record this weight and the note sounded by the string (for example, C or F sharp). Next, add enough sand for the string to make a note one semitone higher. For example, if the starting note was D, then the next note should be D sharp. If you are not sure how to do this, ask the help of someone who can read music. Weigh the bucket and sand again. Repeat this until you have a list of about ten notes and the corresponding weights. Plot your results on a graph. What shape is the curve?

Wave after Wave
The rate at which a sound wave goes back and forth is called the frequency. It is measured in the number of vibrations per second, or hertz. (The German scientist Heinrich Hertz, after which the unit of frequency is named, did a lot of work in the science of waves.)

For example, if a string vibrates 250 times a second it gives rise to a sound wave with a frequency of 250 hertz. An object that vibrates 1,350 times a second produces sound with a frequency of 1,350 hertz, and so on.

If a string of a certain length is stretched tighter it will vibrate faster, producing sound of a higher frequency. Can you suggest a reason why humans and other animals can vary the frequency of the sounds they make?

For more on this, see "Experiment in Depth," page 55, section 1.

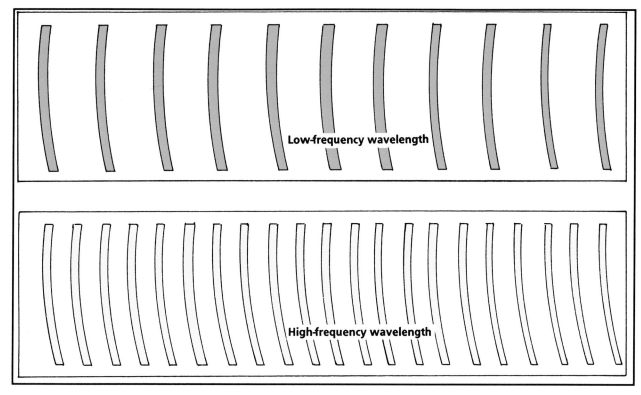

Low-frequency wavelength

High-frequency wavelength

▲ *This drawing shows waves of high frequency and low frequency.*

Probing with Ultrasound

Sound that is too high for humans to hear is known as ultrasound. It has a number of important uses, one of which is the ultrasound scanner. Using this, a doctor can watch a moving television picture of an unborn baby inside its mother. The scanner sends out a beam of ultrasound into the mother's body. It then picks up the echoes that come back from the baby. The returning signals are used to build up a picture on a television screen. Not only does the reflected ultrasound beam show the outline of the whole baby but it also shows details inside the baby such as its beating heart. In this way, the doctor can check if all is well and whether, for example, the mother is carrying one baby or two.

Industries also make use of ultrasound. A beam of ultrasound can check metal parts, such as those of an aircraft, to see if they contain any tiny cracks. More powerful beams can cause materials to vibrate so much that they heat up and melt. Ultrasonic welding machines are used to weld plastic parts together.

CHAPTER 3

Hear, Hear!

There is more to your ear than meets the eye. All you can see from the outside is a folded lobe of skin, known as the outer ear, and a small, dark passage that leads inward. Along this passage, called the ear canal, sounds travel to the more complicated parts of your ear that lie hidden inside your head.

A close-up outside view of a human ear. ▶

Collecting Sounds

You Will Need:

- **A large sheet of paper or cardboard**
- **A plastic funnel**
- **About 3' of plastic tubing**
- **A radio**
- **A ticking watch**

What to Do:

Roll the sheet of paper or cardboard into a cone shape. The cone should be as wide as possible at one end and narrow enough at the other to fit comfortably over the opening of your ear canal. Tape the ends of the cone to hold them in place. Turn the radio on so you can just hear it when standing a few yards away. Hold the cone to your ear and point the wide opening at the radio. What do you notice? Point the cone in a different direction. What happens?

Push the funnel into one end of the plastic tubing. Place the watch on a table. Hold the funnel over the watch and put the other end of the tubing to your ear. Try to explain your results. Point the funnel at other sources of sound, such as people talking some distance away or a car passing by.

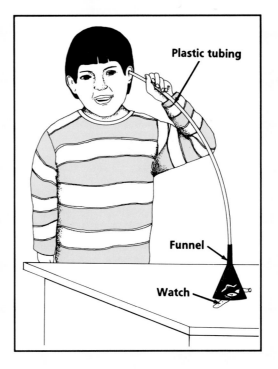

Plastic tubing

Funnel

Watch

Warning: Never push anything deep into your ear canal as this could seriously damage your hearing.

Journey into the Ear

The outer ear helps to collect sound and funnel it into the ear canal. At the end of the canal is a thin, round sheet of skin called the eardrum. This vibrates back and forth when sounds fall upon it.

Connected to the eardrum are three tiny bones named the hammer, the anvil, and the stirrup because of their shapes. These bones make up the middle ear. The stirrup, measuring less than a fifth of an inch in length, is the smallest bone in the human body. Together, the hammer, anvil, and stirrup increase, or amplify, the vibrations of the eardrum and pass them on to the inner ear. Here lies an object known as the cochlea that looks like a snail's shell. The cochlea changes the vibrations it receives into electrical signals which then travel along a special pathway–the auditory nerve–to the brain.

Joined on to the cochlea are three loops, set at right angles to each other.

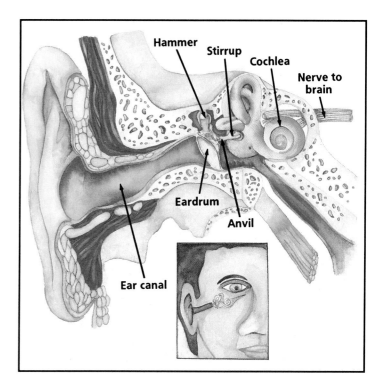

▲ *This diagram shows the parts of the human ear.*

These are the semicircular canals which are filled with liquid and play an important part in our ability to balance.

Ear Tests

You Will Need:

- **A pin**
- **A ruler**
- **A table**
- **A number of volunteers of different ages from young to old**
- **Cotton***

What to Do:

Ask the first volunteer to stand with his or her back to the table. Drop the pin from a height of 6" onto the table. Ask the volunteer to raise a hand if he or she can hear the pin hitting the table. If the volunteer raises a hand, ask him or her to take a step farther away. Carry out the test again. Continue until the person can no longer hear the sound of the pin. Measure his or her distance from the table. Repeat this with each of the remaining volunteers. What are your findings? Plot a graph of distance from the table against age. Does there seem to be any connection between a person's age and his or her ability to hear the pin drop?

In your experiment, can the ▶ volunteer hear the pin drop?

Taking It Further:

Your results will be more meaningful if you can include more people in the test. You might also see what happens if you drop a different kind of object, such as an eraser, from a fixed distance. Do the results change if the sound is of a different pitch or quality?

What happens if you plug one of the ears of each volunteer with cotton? (Be sure to provide a fresh piece of cotton for each volunteer.) How does this affect the distance at which each person can hear the test object fall? Does it affect all ages by the same amount? Write about your findings and try to explain them.

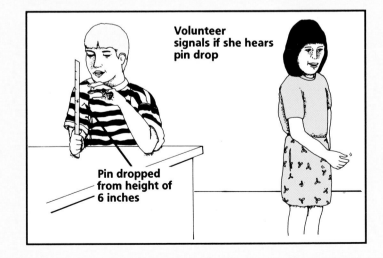

Volunteer signals if she hears pin drop

Pin dropped from height of 6 inches

What Can You Hear?

Humans can hear sounds within a range of frequencies from about 20 hertz (that is, twenty vibrations per second) to about 17,000 hertz. However, as we grow older, both the sharpness of our hearing and our ability to hear very high-pitched sounds decrease.

In addition, we may suffer from a variety of conditions that make us partly or completely deaf. Very loud sounds or a blow on the head may damage the eardrum, or a person may be born with a middle or inner ear that does not work properly. Sometimes this can be helped with a device such as a hearing aid. In other cases, the person may learn to communicate by lip reading and by signing with his or her hands.

*Most people can hear sounds ▶
made by musical instruments.*

Sounds and Directions

You Will Need:

- **Several volunteers**
- **A blindfold**

What to Do:

Blindfold a volunteer and have the rest of your helpers stand around him or her in a circle. Take turns making a quiet sound, such as a snap of the fingers. The person in the center has to point in the direction from which he or she thinks the sound is coming. How good is he or she at finding the correct direction? Repeat the test several times with other volunteers wearing the blindfold. Are some people better than others at pinpointing the direction of sounds? What happens if the person in the center puts a cotton plug in one of his or her ears? Does this make his or her ability to tell the direction of sounds better or worse? Can you explain your results?

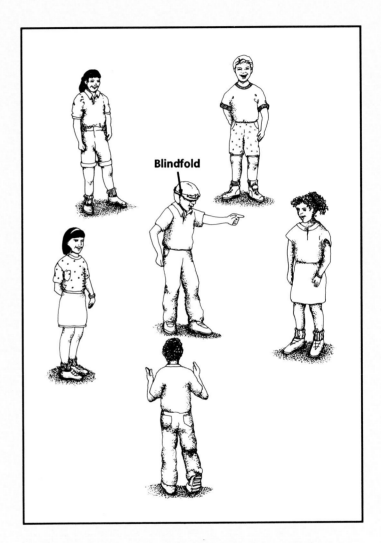

▲ *Can a person wearing the blindfold tell from which directions sounds are coming?*

Hearing Aids and Implants

A hearing aid works simply by picking up sounds from outside and then making them louder or clearer so that the wearer can hear better or more clearly. But a hearing aid is no use to someone who cannot hear at all. A new device, however, known as a cochlear implant, means that even some totally deaf people can be given a sense of hearing. The cochlear implant consists of a tiny, flat radio receiver and a long tail containing one or more very fine wires. During an operation, the receiver is placed beneath the skin, just behind the ear. The long tail is pushed inside the curl of the snail-shaped cochlea. Outside the ear is a microphone that picks up sound and passes it to a miniature computer. This computer changes the sounds to pulses of electricity which are passed to the radio receiver and then on to the cochlea. The most advanced implants available at pres-

▲ *A hearing aid helps people who need sounds made louder or clearer.*

ent sort the incoming sounds into as many as twenty-two different bands, according to their frequency, and send each of these to a different point on the cochlea.

Noise and Concentration

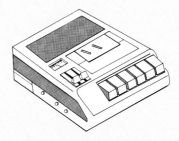

You Will Need:

- A radio
- A tape recorder
- A music tape
- A book
- A desk and chair
- A stopwatch
- Several volunteers

What to Do:

Choose three different passages from a book and prepare ten questions on each. The passages should be short enough that they can each be read in about a minute.

Ask the first volunteer to sit at the desk. Make sure the room is quiet. Put the first passage in front of the person and allow him or her exactly one minute, as measured by the stopwatch, to read it. When the time is up, close the book and ask the ten prepared questions, noting the volunteer's replies. Next, turn on the radio between stations so that you can hear a loud hiss of "static." Make a note of the volume setting on the radio. Allow the volunteer to study the second passage for one minute and again record the answers to your ten questions. Finally, switch on the tape recorder playing loud pop music. Give the volunteer the third passage and after one minute ask the third set of questions. Repeat the experiment with several other people, making sure that the conditions are the same for each. Add up the total number of correct answers for each passage in the book and divide by the number of volunteers to obtain the average score. What do you find? Do your results suggest that the ability of people to concentrate is affected by noise? Which noise, if any, seems to have the greatest effect—the hiss of the untuned radio or the taped music?

Taking It Further:

There are many ways to extend this test. For example, you could investigate whether people's concentration is more affected by loud rock music or loud classical music. Does television have a greater affect than a stereo playing at the same volume? Are people's abilities to perform other tasks—doing a jigsaw puzzle, shooting baskets, and so on—influenced by noise? Design your own experiments to answer some of these questions.

For more on this, see "Experiment in Depth," page 55, section 2.

Believe It or Not!

THE GREAT GERMAN COMPOSER, LUDWIG VAN BEETHOVEN, WAS TOTALLY DEAF WHEN HE WROTE HIS NINTH SYMPHONY. AT THE FIRST PERFORMANCE HE WAS STILL CONDUCTING AFTER THE ORCHESTRA HAD FINISHED.

CHAPTER 4

Making Music

▲ *These symphony musicians are playing classical music.*

Jazz, opera, rock, soul–music comes in an amazing variety of forms. It is played in every country on earth, to relax, to rejoice, to dance, or to march by. But what is the difference between sounds that are musical and those that are not?

Music is a series of sounds arranged so that people–or some people, at least–enjoy them. The basic building blocks of musical sounds are notes. In these, the sound waves vibrate in a regular and repetitive way. A noise, on the other hand, is made up of sound waves that have no regular pattern.

Strums, Hums, and Drums
Music can be made in many different ways.

Some instruments, like the guitar, have strings that are plucked. Others have strings that are stroked with a bow. Wind instruments, such as flutes, trumpets, and saxophones, are played by blowing into them. Others, including xylophones and drums, make musical sounds when they are struck.

All instruments have their own special sound by which they can be recognized.

Same Note, Different Sound

You Will Need:

- **A variety of musical instruments and people who can play them**
- **Several blindfolded volunteers**

What to Do:

Ask each musician to play (in turn) the same note—for example, middle C—on his or her instrument. After each note, ask the blindfolded volunteer to say which instrument, from a list of possible choices, has just sounded. Repeat the test with other volunteers. What are the results? Did any instruments prove especially hard to identify? Why do you think this should be?

Do the experiment again, but this time ask the musicians to sound the note in pairs. For example, a piano and a flute might play the same note together, or a clarinet and a guitar. In each case, the musicians should try to play at the same volume. Ask each volunteer to say which two instruments are playing. How well do the volunteers score? Which instrument pairs do they have most difficulty in identifying?*

*For more on this, see "Experiment in Depth," pages 55-56, section 3.

▲ *A musician plays a trumpet by blowing into the end of the instrument.*

Even when the same note is played on two different instruments–a clarinet and a trombone, for example–we can tell them apart. The reason is that each instrument, as well as producing a basic note, also gives off a wide assortment of other, related notes at the same time. It is these many accompanying sounds which, together with the basic note, create the unique sound quality, or timbre, of each instrument.

The Sounds of Music

All string instruments have a set of stretched strings or wires. These vibrate at different rates depending on their length and tightness. The vibration of a string causes the whole body of the instrument to vibrate. This results in a much louder sound. A violin and guitar have only a few strings, so the musician must hold down the strings in various positions to play all the possible notes of the instrument. A

Playing Science

You Will Need:

- **A plastic recorder (or penny whistle)**
- **A jug of water**
- **Two drinking straws**
- **Scissors**
- **Several glass bottles of the same size**
- **A wooden spoon**
- **A piano**

What to Do:
Cover all the holes on the recorder with your fingers. Blow gently into it and listen to the pitch of the sound it makes. Take a deep breath and blow into the recorder while you push it into the jug of water. What happens to the pitch of the note? Take another breath and blow again while you pull the recorder out of the water. Can you explain what you hear?

Flatten the end of one straw and snip off the corners as shown in the diagram. Hold the cut end lightly between your lips and blow gently. What happens? Cut off half the straw. How does the sound change? Prepare the end of another straw in the same way. Take a deep breath and, as you blow

Flatten end of straw

Cut off ends like this

into the straw, quickly snip off short sections from the end. With practice you may even be able to play a scale.

Fill the bottles with water to different heights. Tap each bottle gently in turn with the wooden spoon. What do you notice? Try to tune the bottles to some of the notes on a piano. Blow across the open top of the bottles. Compare these sounds with those produced by tapping.

Ask an adult to show you the inside of a piano. What happens when one of the keys is pressed? How is the sound produced? What happens when the various pedals of the instrument are pushed down? How many strings are there for each key on the keyboard? Why should this be? Try holding all but one of the strings while someone presses the corresponding key. How does this affect the sound?

Blow across top of bottle

Tap with wooden spoon

▲ *What sounds can you make with a recorder in and out of water or with straws?*
◄ *What sounds can you make by blowing across the top of bottles of water?*

▲ *A violin and a piano are both string instruments.*

piano or harp, on the other hand, contains one or more strings for every note.

Blowing into a wind instrument, such as a flute, causes a column of air to vibrate. The length of this column determines the pitch of the note–the longer the column, the deeper the sound. For example, if you cover just the top hole of a recorder, the note is high because the air can vibrate only as far as the next open hole. However, if you cover all the holes, the note is low because the air can now vibrate through-out the whole length of the instrument. Some wind instruments, in order to pro-

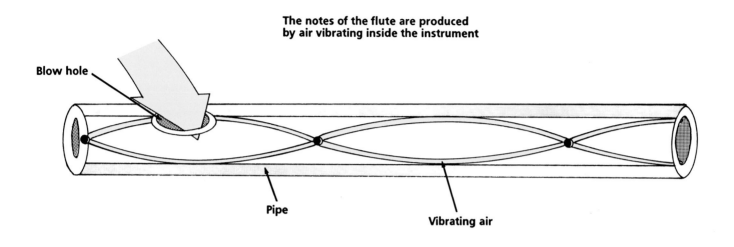

The notes of the flute are produced by air vibrating inside the instrument

Blow hole

Pipe

Vibrating air

▲ *The notes of a flute are produced by air vibrating inside the instrument.*

duce very low notes, have such long tubes that they must be bent around several times. The coiled brass piping of a tube, for instance, measures over twelve feet in length.

A percussion instrument, such as a xylophone or drum, works in the simplest possible way. Its playing surface is struck and caused to vibrate directly.

Good Listening

Sounds inside a room travel not just directly to your ears, but also after bouncing off the walls, floor, and ceiling. If these surfaces are hard and bare–as they often are in a church, for example–any sounds you hear may seem harsh and confused. If you ever moved from your house you may have noticed how much the rooms echo

A Model Concert Hall

You Will Need:

- An empty, bare room
- Old sheets, rugs, padded chairs, cushions
- A tape recorder and music tape
- A table

What to Do:
Place the tape recorder on a table against one wall of the room. Turn on the recorder so that it plays at a fairly high volume. Stand at the back of the room and listen to the sound. How would you describe it? Is it harsh or mellow? Why should this be?

Bring some items such as a rug, a few padded chairs, and some sheets into the room. Ask an adult to help you hang the sheets against one or two of the walls. Play the recorded music again. Has the sound changed? In what way? Experiment with other arrangements of wall and floor coverings and items about the room. How is the quality of sound affected? Try to achieve the best possible sound—not too harsh and not too muffled. Does the sound quality vary from one part of the room to another?

when they are empty of furniture, curtains, and carpets.

In the case of a concert hall, the quality of sound reaching the audience's ears is all-important. For this reason, great care has to be taken in designing the shape of the room and the materials that cover the walls, ceiling, and floor.

Synthetic Sound

A synthesizer can produce the sound of a church organ, of breaking glass, of a trumpet, or of weird sounds no human ear has ever heard before. To synthesize means to put together. So a synthesizer is an instrument that can build complex sounds from simpler ones. It uses a computer to create and store sounds electronically. These sounds can then be called up and played–usually by pressing the keys of a keyboard that is connected to the synthesizer.

An extension of the synthesizer is the

▲ *A concert hall is designed to project the sounds of musical instruments to the audience.*

"sampler." This can record real sounds, such as those of a drum or an electric guitar, and convert them into series of numbers which are stored by a computer. Samplers are used in recording studios to capture the sounds made by separate instruments and singers. Recordings of a number of performances are made and, from these, the best parts are put together and improved electronically. Strange as it seems, none of today's hit records were ever played as you hear them.

Believe It or Not!

OOPS!

WOODEN-FRAMED PIANOS HAVE BEEN KNOWN TO SNAP IN HALF WHILE BEING TUNED BECAUSE WHEN FULLY TIGHTENED THE PULL OF ALL THE STRINGS MAY BE MORE THAN TWENTY TONS.

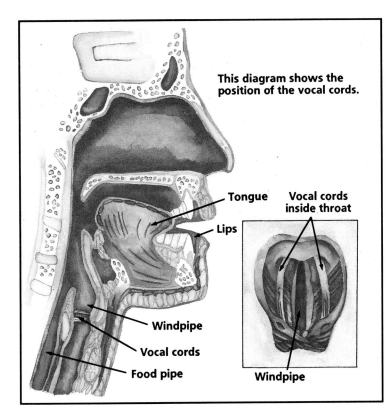

This diagram shows the position of the vocal cords.

Tongue

Vocal cords inside throat

Lips

Windpipe

Vocal cords

Food pipe

Windpipe

▲ *This diagram shows the human throat and vocal cords.*

The Human Voice

If you touch the front of your neck while you say something, you will be able to feel your throat vibrating. This is because you have two flaps of skin inside your throat called vocal cords. When you speak or sing, air from your lungs is forced over the vocal cords causing them to vibrate. In turn, this makes the air in your throat and mouth vibrate at the same rate. Muscles in the throat stretch the vocal cords tighter to make higher sounds and relax them to make deeper tones. Women generally have higher voices than men because their vocal cords are shorter. The basic sound from the vocal cords can be altered a great deal through movements of the mouth, tongue, and lips. In this way, we can produce all of the many variations of sound in human languages.

Blow Your Own Horn

What to Do:
Lightly touch your neck while you hum a note. Now hum a higher note, followed by a lower note. Can you feel any change? If so, can you explain what may have moved? As you hum, press gently several times against your neck. Does the sound change? Why should that be? Open your mouth wide and make a sound without moving your mouth. This is the basic sound produced by your vocal cords. Now try moving your mouth, tongue, and lips in different ways. Listen to the variety of sounds that come out.

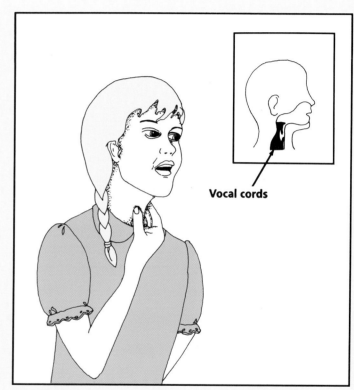

Vocal cords

▲ *What kinds of sounds can you make as you hum?*

Through the Sound Barrier

Strange though it may seem, all the sounds you can hear were made in the past. The reason for this is that it takes sound waves time to travel from one place to another. So, any sound reaching your ears now began its journey a short while ago—in the past.

▲ *The sounds produced by a supersonic air-craft may take seconds to reach the ground.*

The Speed of Sound

You Will Need:

- A large, quiet area of open ground
- A long tape measure
- A stopwatch
- Binoculars
- Two metal bars
- An assistant

What to Do:

Measure a distance of 1,500 feet as accurately as possible. Ask your assistant to stand at one end of the marked distance holding a metal bar in each hand. Stand at the other end, holding the stopwatch and watching your assistant through the binoculars. When you shout "Go!" your assistant should crash the two bars together above his or her head, as loudly as possible. As soon as you see the two bars meet, start the watch and as soon as you hear the sound, stop the watch. Record the time to the nearest tenth of a second. Repeat this ten times. Find the average time by adding up all the measured times and dividing by ten. To work out the approximate speed of sound, divide the distance (1,500 feet) by your average time.

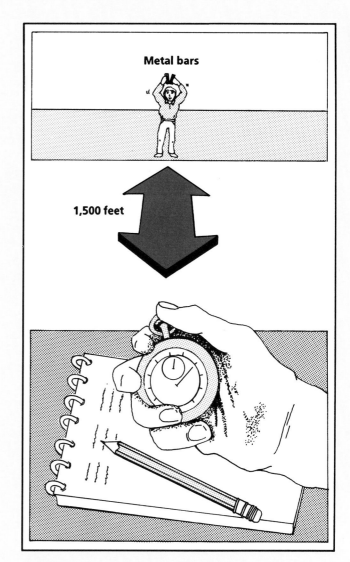

Metal bars

1,500 feet

▲ What do you learn about light and sound from this experiment?

The sound of thunder reaches the observer in about 15 seconds

Storm Cloud

Light reaches the observer in 16 millionths of a second

Lightning Strike

An observer, 3 miles away, sees lightning flash about 15 seconds before hearing thunder

▲ *This diagram shows how the light from lightning reaches a person before the sound from thunder.*

Thunder and Lightning

The speed of sound in air, under normal conditions, is about 1,100 feet per second or 750 miles per hour. That may seem fast, but it is about a million times slower than the speed of light (which is over 186,000 miles per second). This big difference between the speed of sound and the speed of light explains why we normally see lightning well before the thunder that was created at the same time. If a storm is two miles away, the flash of lightning from it will reach us in less than one ten-thousandth of a second—that is, almost instantly. However, the rumble of the accompanying noise will take over nine

▲ *Because light travels faster than sound, we see lightning before we hear thunder.*

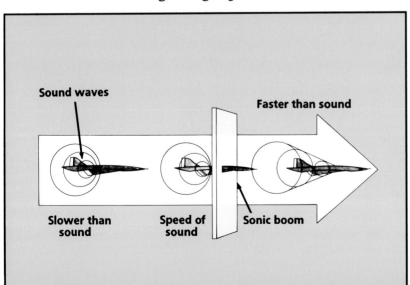

Sound waves

Faster than sound

Slower than sound

Speed of sound

Sonic boom

seconds to travel the same distance. In fact, by measuring the interval between the thunder and the lightning, we can work out roughly how far the storm is from us.

Sonic Booms

A supersonic aircraft, such as the Concorde, is one that can travel faster than the speed of sound. As the plane approaches the speed of sound, it catches up with the sound waves traveling in front of it and pushes them up against each other. The result is a barrier of squashed air in front of the aircraft. As the plane reaches the speed of sound, it breaks through this barrier and causes the squashed air to spread out rapidly behind in a powerful "shock wave." When the shock wave reaches the ground, people hear a noise like a loud clap of thunder. This so-called sonic boom may have enough force to shatter windows.

◄ *This diagram shows how a supersonic aircraft creates a sonic boom.*

A Change of Pitch

You Will Need:

- **A quiet area of open ground, such as a park**
- **A bicycle**
- **A whistle**
- **An assistant**

What to Do:

Ask the assistant to take a deep breath and blow the whistle steadily while you ride quickly toward and past him or her on the bicycle. What happens to the sound of the whistle as you go past? Can you think of any way to explain what happens?

Whistle

▲ *What do you learn about sound from this experiment?*

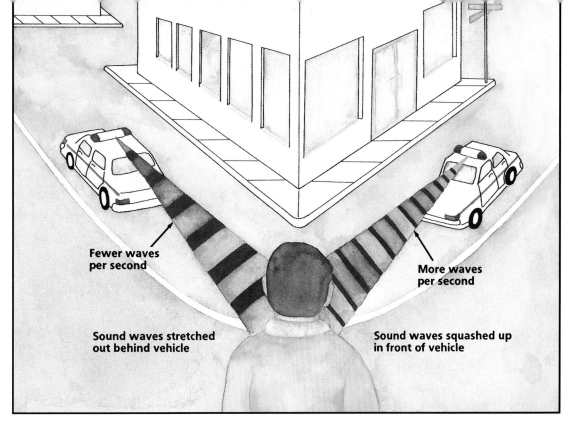

Fewer waves
per second

More waves
per second

Sound waves stretched
out behind vehicle

Sound waves squashed up
in front of vehicle

▲ *How does the Doppler effect affect the way a person hears the sound from the siren of a police car or ambulance?*

The Doppler Effect

As a police car or ambulance passes you, with its siren wailing, the sound of the siren seems to drop to a lower note. This is due to something known as the Doppler effect, named after the Austrian scientist Christian Johann Doppler, who discovered the reason for it in 1842.

Doppler found that if a source of sound is moving, the sound waves are crowded together in front of it and spread apart behind it. Squeezing sound waves together increases their frequency, while spreading them lowers their frequency. As a result, to someone at rest the sound will seem higher when the source is approaching and lower when it is moving away.

At the time when Doppler announced his findings, there was no easy means to test them. The fastest form of transport which carried a horn was the horse-drawn mail coach. This only moved at about ten miles an hour–too slow for the Doppler effect to be noticeable. It was only in 1845, when a scientist took a trumpet aboard a train locomotive, that the effect was first demonstrated.

CHAPTER 6

Animal Chatter

Among the most unusual and varied sounds on earth are those made by animals. Monkeys chatter and shriek, birds chirrup and squawk, and bullfrogs produce an amazingly loud noise to attract mates and drive away other males during the breeding season.

The bullfrog passes air back and forth from its mouth to its lungs across its vocal cords. Some of the air goes into special sacs at the bottom of the mouth. These sacs then blow up like a balloon and act like a sound box to amplify the vibrations of the vocal cords.

Most animal sounds, like those of the bullfrog, serve as a form of communication. They may warn, attract, or help an

A green monkey shrieks out a ▶ loud message for other monkeys.

individual to identify itself to others nearby.

Whales and dolphins produce an especially complex variety of sounds. So much so that some scientists have suggested they may have an advanced language of their own. What is certain is that these creatures can call to one another with sounds that are both below and above the range of human hearing. Dolphins seem to have another use for the ultrasonic "clicks" they are capable of producing. With a powerful, narrow beam of ultrasound they can stun a fish and then grab it in their jaws before it has a chance to recover.

Strange Sounds, Strange Ears

Many animal sounds are not produced in the throat but by other parts of a creature's body. The hum of a hummingbird, for instance, is caused by the rapid beating of the bird's wings–up to fifty times a second in some species. These continuous wing movements set up vibrations in the

Capturing Animals on Tape

You Will Need:

- A tape recorder
- A microphone
- An umbrella*
- Tape*
- Headphones*

What to Do:
Place the tape recorder and microphone outside in the area you are interested in. This might be, for example, a flower bed visited by bees or tall grass in which crickets live. Turn on the recorder and wait some distance away. After you have made the recording, add a short commentary that includes the date and place of the recording and the weather conditions. Some animals perform only under certain conditions and your tapes will be of much greater value if you record full information.

Taking It Further:
Observe closely the behavior and habits of the animal you wish to record. This will help you to set up your equipment in the best position and at the best time of day.

Another way to improve the quality of your recordings is to attach the microphone to the stem of an umbrella, as shown. The umbrella acts like a large sound-gathering dish. It focuses the sound waves coming from a particular direction to a single point. Hold the microphone against the stem of the

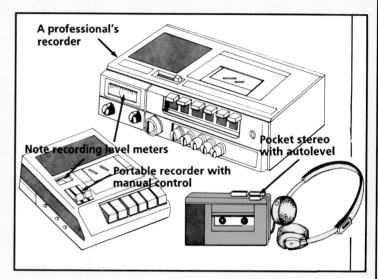

A professional's recorder

Note recording level meters

Portable recorder with manual control

Pocket stereo with autolevel

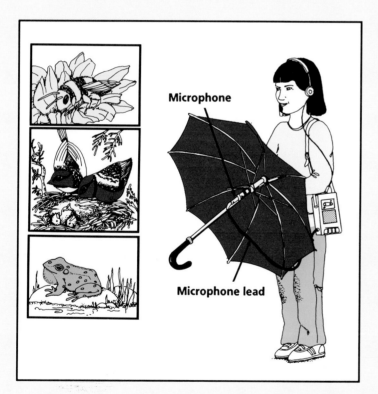

Microphone

Microphone lead

▲ *What kinds of animal sounds can you record?*

umbrella, facing into the dish, about 6" from the top. To position the microphone exactly at the focus of the dish, use headphones attached to the tape recorder so that you can monitor the sounds being picked up. Point the umbrella stem at a distance to the source of the sound and adjust the microphone's position until the sound seems loudest, then tape the microphone to the stem. Using this equipment it should be possible to record the sounds of a single animal, such as a bird singing in a tree, even if it is a hundred yards or more away.

For more on this, see "Experiment in Depth," page 56, section 4.

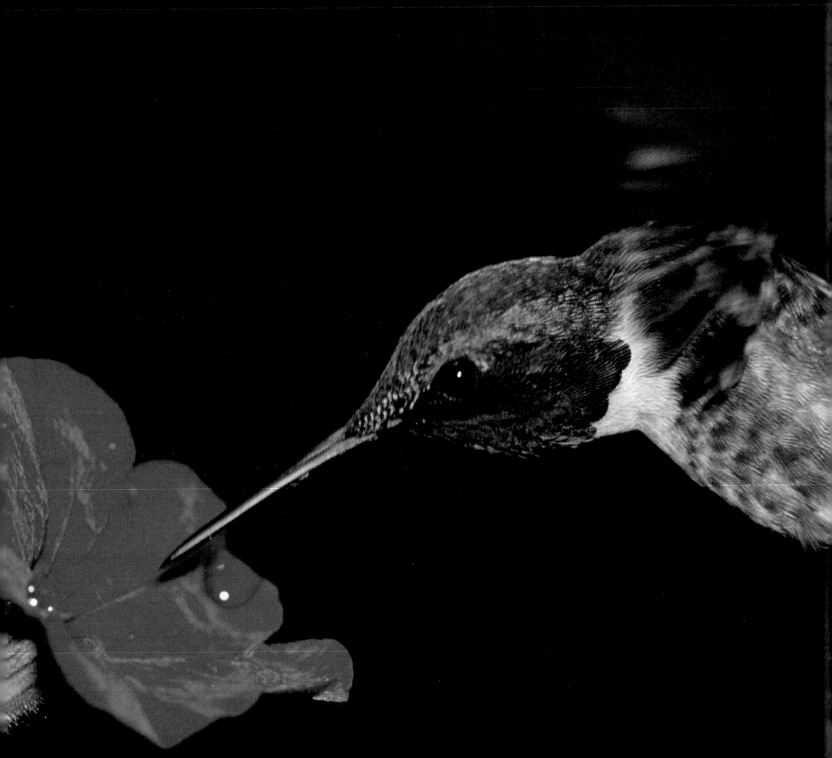

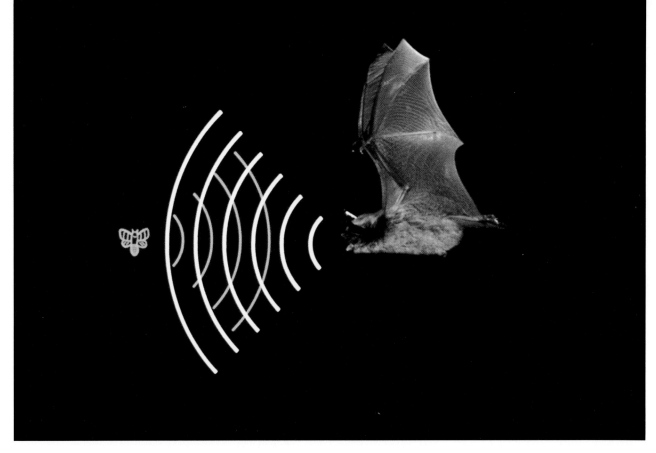

▲ *A bat uses waves of ultrasound to locate insects in flight.*

surrounding air which reach our ears as the familiar low-pitch drone. If you have hummingbirds in your area, set up a feeder and listen to how the note of a hummingbird's hum changes as the bird stretches its beak forward to feed.

As well as producing sounds in unusual ways, animals may also have ears in the oddest places. A grasshopper, for example, picks up sound through two slitlike openings just below the first joint in its front legs. The sound then travels to two small air pockets, the vibrations of which are detected by a sensitive lining.

◄ *The rapid beating of a hummingbird's wings creates a loud hum.*

Sounding Out Prey

Several animals use sound rather than sight to find their way and their food. Most bats sleep by day and hunt by night. As they fly, they give off high-pitched squeaks, usually beyond the range of human hearing. The waves of ultrasound from the bat bounce off obstacles and insects and return to the animal's large, sensitive ears. From the echoes, the bat is able to work out the exact distance and direction of whatever lies in its path. Ultrasound produces a much sharper view than ordinary sound waves would. Dolphins also use this method, known as echolocation, to find their prey.

Believe It or Not!

THE CALL OF THE HUMPBACK WHALE IS THE LOUDEST NOISE MADE BY ANY LIVING CREATURE. AT 190 DECIBELS IT IS LOUDER THAN A CONCORDE JETLINER DURING TAKEOFF.

This section looks at some of the experiments described in this book in more detail.

1. Higher and Higher, pages 19-20. This experiment, and several others in this book, will be simpler to carry out if you have access to a sound frequency meter. This is an instrument that automatically displays the frequency of a note.

With a frequency meter, you can measure directly the frequency of sound produced by the stretched line each time you increase the load hanging from it.

Try repeating the experiment with a nylon line of a different thickness. Is the curve you obtain the same?

2. Noise and Concentration, pages 30-31. This experiment, or series of experiments, could be developed into a science fair project. Among some questions that such a project might try to answer: Does background noise, such as that of a television, affect a person's ability to do homework? Can we concentrate better in total silence or with some quiet, soothing sounds going on? Does very loud noise affect our reaction time–that is, the speed with which we can respond to a sudden signal?

3. Same Note, Different Sound, page 33. The best way to study the differences in sound produced by various musical instruments is with a microphone connected to a device called an oscilloscope. Perhaps a demonstration using this equipment could be set up in your school laboratory. An oscilloscope will show the shape of the sound waves picked up by a microphone. It also allows you to measure the frequencies at which most of the sound is being given off. How does this differ from one instrument to another? How does the shape of the sound wave change if the note is played louder or softer?

Use the oscilloscope to look at the pattern of sound waves in your own voice. Try saying different words or vowel sounds. Compare your "voice patterns" with those of other people. Can you see any differences?

Compare the appearance of the sound wave of a noise, such as hands clapping, with that of the note from a tuning fork.

4. Capturing Animals on Tape, pages 50-51. Noise is always a problem when recording outside, and it is often worse than we think because our ears and brains are very good at cutting out unimportant sounds. A microphone, on the other hand, picks them all up. Wind is the biggest nuisance, but this can be partly overcome by putting some fine material over the microphone. The material must be held away from the end of the microphone–for example, by a wire frame.

The quality of recordings depends much upon the quality of the recording equipment. Most cassette recorders have an automatic volume control, but this can be a disadvantage for wildlife recording because animal sounds often come in sudden bursts. This does not give an automatic system a chance to adjust itself. A recorder with a manual recording level control is better since you can adjust it to the volume of sound it is picking up.

Many types of microphones are available. They vary in shape, size, sensitivity, and cost. The best for general use is a cardioid microphone, also called a unidirectional microphone. It tends to dampen out sounds not coming from the direction in which it is pointed so it is especially useful for recording birds.

GLOSSARY

cochlea—a snail-shaped structure in the inner ear in which sound vibrations are changed to electrical signals before being sent to the brain

cochlear implant—a device that is placed inside the ear during an operation. Part of the cochlear implant picks up sounds outside the ear and changes them to electrical signals. These then travel along fine wires to the cochlea.

Doppler effect—the effect by which sound (or light) waves are crowded together if their source is moving toward, you and spread apart if the source is moving away

ear canal—the passage leading from the outer ear to the eardrum

eardrum—the thin, oval-shaped piece of skin which lies at the boundary between the outer and middle ear. It vibrates at the same frequency as the sounds which fall upon it.

echo—a sound that has bounced back off a hard surface to be heard shortly after the original sound

energy—the ability to do work or cause movement

frequency—the number of times a wave vibrates in a second

hertz—the unit of frequency. One hertz equals one vibration (or "cycle") per second.

inner ear—a connected series of tubes and passageways in the skull which includes the cochlea and semicircular canals

middle ear—an air-filled space which contains a chain of three tiny bones—the hammer, anvil, and stirrup. These transmit the vibrations of the eardrum to the inner ear.

outer ear—the part of the ear you can see from the outside, together with the ear canal

pitch—the highness or lowness of a sound

sampler—an electronic device that can record real sounds and store them in the form of series of numbers. These stored sounds can then be combined or altered using a built-in computer.

semi-circular canals—three looped tubes in the inner ear that are joined together and contain a special liquid. They play an important part in our sense of balance.

sonar—a method of finding the distance and speed of an object by bouncing sound waves off it

sonic boom—the loud noise made by a plane or other object as it goes past the speed of sound. It is caused by the plane breaking through the compressed air waves that built up ahead of it.

supersonic—meaning "greater than the speed of sound"

synthesizer—an instrument that can create almost any sound by combining simple sounds electronically

timbre—the quality of a sound made by a musical instrument. It depends on the mixture of the basic note with other frequencies that are present.

ultrasound—sound that is too high in frequency to be heard by the human ear

vocal cords—the stretched pieces of skin in the human throat which vibrate and make sounds when air from the lungs is forced over them

INDEX

About the Author

Dr. David Darling is the author of many science books for young readers, including the Dillon Press Discovering Our Universe, World of Computers, and Could You Ever? series. Dr. Darling, who holds degrees in physics and astronomy, has also written many articles for *Astronomy* and *Odyssey* magazines. His first science book for adult readers, *Deep Time* (1989), has been described by Arthur C. Clarke as "brilliant." He currently lives with his family in England, where he writes and lectures to students in schools.